Team Spirit®

THE PITTSBURGH PENGUINS

BY

MARK STEWART

Content Consultant
Denis Gibbons
Society for International Hockey Research

NORWOOD HOUSE PRESS

CHICAGO, ILLINOIS

Norwood House Press
P.O. Box 316598
Chicago, Illinois 60631

For information regarding Norwood House Press, please visit our website at:
www.norwoodhousepress.com or call 866-565-2900.

PHOTO CREDITS:
All photos courtesy Getty Images except the following:
Author's Collection (6, 40 bottom), O-Pee-Chee/Hockey Hall of Fame (8),
Topps, Inc. (7, 9, 14, 21, 29, 35 top left, 37, 41 right, 43),
Associated Press (16, 23), Beckett Media LLC (17, 40 top left),
NHLPA (20, 34 left), National Hockey League Services (22),
Black Book Partners (26, 41 left),
Sports Illustrated/TIME Inc. (27), Icon SMI (31, 36),
The Hockey News/W.C.C. Publishing Ltd. (34 right, 35 top right),
The National Hockey League (38), ESPN The Magazine (40 bottom left),
Matt Richman (48).
Cover photo: Jamie Sabau/Getty Images
Special thanks to Topps, Inc.

Editor: Mike Kennedy
Designer: Ron Jaffe
Project Management: Black Book Partners, LLC.
Research: Joshua Zaffos
Special thanks to Jan Paul Matthews

LIBRARY OF CONGRESS CATALOGING-IN-PUBLICATION DATA

Stewart, Mark, 1960-
    The Pittsburgh Penguins / by Mark Stewart.
        p. cm. -- (Team spirit)
    Includes bibliographical references and index.
    Summary: "Presents the history and accomplishments of the Pittsburgh
Penguins hockey team. Includes highlights of players, coaches, and awards,
quotes, timeline, maps, glossary and websites"--Provided by publisher.
    ISBN-13: 978-1-59953-340-7 (library edition : alk. paper)
    ISBN-10: 1-59953-340-5 (library edition : alk. paper) 1. Pittsburgh
Penguins (Hockey team)--History--Juvenile literature. I. Title.
    GV848.P58S75 2009
    796.962'640974886--dc22
                                                    2009018711

Manufactured in the United States of America in North Mankato, Minnesota.
155R-022010

COVER PHOTO: The Penguins enjoy a wild celebration after winning the
Stanley Cup in 2008–09.

Table of Contents

SPORTS WORDS & VOCABULARY WORDS: In this book, you will find many words that are new to you. You may also see familiar words used in new ways. The glossary on page 46 gives the meanings of hockey words, as well as "everyday" words that have special hockey meanings. These words appear in **bold type** throughout the book. The glossary on page 47 gives the meanings of vocabulary words that are not related to hockey. They appear in ***bold italic type*** throughout the book.

Meet the Penguins

To win a game in the **National Hockey League (NHL)**, a team must have great focus and tremendous heart. Every player must work his hardest every moment he is on the ice. When both teams give their maximum effort, talent will usually win out. The Pittsburgh Penguins know all about talent.

The Penguins have had some of the greatest players in NHL history. In fact, for about two *decades*, they had a player that some say was the greatest ever. During that *era*, the team learned that surrounding a superstar with solid **role players** was the key to winning the **Stanley Cup**.

This book tells the story of the Penguins. The team has enjoyed incredible triumph and endured heartbreaking tragedy. Few NHL clubs have had higher highs or lower lows. And no team in modern times is more exciting when the Penguins are at their best.

Evgeni Malkin, Sidney Crosby, and Brooks Orpik congratulate
Sergei Gonchar after a goal during a 2008–09 game.

Way Back When

During the 1940s and 1950s, the NHL had only six teams. Competition was fierce for the Stanley Cup, and the talent on every team was tremendous. For the 1967–68 season, the league doubled in size to 12 teams. One of the new teams was the Penguins. The NHL knew Pittsburgh was a good hockey town. A **minor-league** team called the Hornets already played there, and fans all over the city supported them.

1967 - Pittsburgh Penguins - 1968

ABOVE: A souvenir photo from the Penguins' first season.
RIGHT: Lowell MacDonald, a member of the "Century Line."

The Penguins built their team with *experienced* players—including Andy Bathgate, Ab McDonald, Ken Schinkel, Bryan Watson, and Leo Boivin. Pittsburgh's goalie was Les Binkley. In his first year, he allowed fewer than three goals per game and was second in the league with six **shutouts**. The Penguins were headed for the **playoffs** until Binkley broke his hand. They fell short by one victory.

LOWELL MacDONALD • L.WING

In the years that followed, the Penguins brought a lot of good, young talent to the ice. Michel Briere was one of the top **rookies** in the NHL in 1969–70. He led Pittsburgh to the playoffs for the first time. A year later, Briere's life was tragically cut short by a car accident.

The Penguins found more good young players in Greg Polis, Dave Burrows, Pierre Larouche, Lowell MacDonald, Jean Pronovost, Rick Kehoe, and Randy Carlyle. Their best player during the 1970s was Syl Apps Jr. His father had been a star for the Toronto Maple Leafs in the 1930s and 1940s. Apps, MacDonald, and Pronovost played together on Pittsburgh's "Century Line."

In the late 1970s, the Penguins traded **draft choices** for **veterans**, but this *strategy* didn't work. For six years in a row during the 1980s,

KEVIN STEVENS • LW

the Penguins failed to reach the playoffs. The news wasn't all bad. In 1984, Pittsburgh chose Mario Lemieux with the first pick in the draft. Lemieux was bigger and stronger than most NHL players. Yet he could skate, pass, and shoot like someone half his size. Opponents were helpless to stop him.

The Penguins built a great team around "Super Mario." Their stars included Jaromir Jagr, Kevin Stevens, Paul Coffey, Bryan Trottier, Ron Francis, and goalie Tom Barrasso. The team was run by Craig Patrick, who came from one of hockey's most famous families. Pittsburgh won the Stanley Cup in 1991 and again in 1992.

Unfortunately, Lemieux was hit hard by health problems, including a bout with cancer, a heart condition, and back and hip injuries. Jagr, however, blossomed into a superstar. In 1995–96, the two combined to form the league's most dangerous scoring duo. Lemieux retired a year later.

In 1998–99, the Penguins fell into serious financial trouble. Lemieux stepped in and bought the team. He was determined to rebuild the Penguins into a Stanley Cup team with a new *generation* of stars.

LEFT: Mario Lemieux, the greatest player in Penguins history.
ABOVE: Kevin Stevens, a star for the team during the 1990s.

The Team Today

In 2000, Mario Lemieux returned to the ice as the owner and star center of the Penguins. Over the next few years, he was able to straighten out the team's business. He also served as the leader of a new group of *emerging* stars. Pittsburgh's young players skated with a legend—it was a big thrill and a great learning experience.

Lemieux retired again during the 2005–06 season. By then, Sidney Crosby was ready to take command of the Penguins. The teenage center was one of the best players in the NHL. Other young Pittsburgh stars included Russian **playmaker** Evgeni Malkin, lightning-fast goalie Marc-Andre Fleury, and a big, strong center named Jordan Staal.

With veteran players like Sergei Gonchar and Petr Sykora providing extra leadership, the Penguins made it back to the **Stanley Cup Finals**. When the siren sounded to end the 2008–09 season, the Penguins were champions again. It was one of the most *remarkable* turnarounds in sports history. Now Pittsburgh fans can hardly wait for each new season to start.

Evgeni Malkin and the rest of the Penguins celebrate as Sidney Crosby raises the Stanley Cup in 2009.

Home Ice

Beginning in their first season, the Penguins played in the Civic Center, which fans called the "Igloo." It was built in 1961 for the Civic Light Opera. The Igloo was the first indoor sports arena with a *retractable* roof. The roof stayed closed for hockey games, but it could slide open for music concerts and other summertime events.

The Igloo got its nickname because of its round shape. Its roof has eight sections and is held up by a huge arch. At one time, three of the sections on each side of the arch could fold under the fourth section.

For the 2010–11 season, the Penguins prepared to move into a new arena. Although the Igloo has some of the best views in the NHL, it is also among the league's smallest arenas. Pittsburgh's new arena offers more seats and a chance for the fans to be even louder.

BY THE NUMBERS

- *The Penguins' arena has 16,940 seats for hockey.*
- *It cost $22 million to build in 1961.*
- *The roof is 415 feet across at its widest point.*
- *As of 2009, the Penguins had retired two numbers—#21 (Michel Briere) and #66 (Mario Lemieux). Wayne Gretzky's #99 has also been retired by every NHL team.*

Marc-Andre Fleury skates behind his net during a 2008–09 game in the Penguins' arena.

Dressed for Success

The Penguins selected their name from thousands of entries in a contest for fans. Some say the name was chosen because of the team's arena, the Igloo. That may be true, though igloos are found in the Arctic, while penguins are found in the Antarctic.

The team's first *logo* featured a penguin with a hockey stick and scarf. It was skating across a triangle, which represented a famous area in Pittsburgh called the Golden Triangle. During the 1990s, the Penguins changed to a more modern logo, but the team returned to its *classic* look in 2000–01.

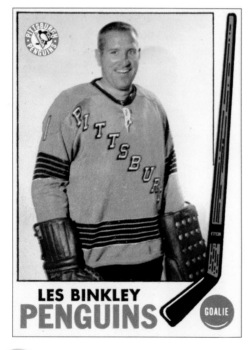

The team's first uniform was light blue with lettering running diagonally across the front. In 1980, the Penguins switched to a new black-and-gold combination. The colors came from Pittsburgh's city crest, and fans all over the area love them. The Steelers football team and Pirates baseball team also use black and gold.

Les Binkley models the team's uniform from the 1960s.

14

UNIFORM BASICS

The hockey uniform has five important parts:
- Helmet
- Sweater
- Pants
- Gloves
- Skates

Hockey helmets are made of hard plastic with softer padding inside. Some players also wear visors to protect their eyes.

The hockey uniform top is called a sweater. Players wear padding underneath it to protect their shoulders, spine, and ribs. Padded hockey pants, or "breezers," extend from the waist to the knees. Players also wear padding on their knees and shins.

Hockey gloves protect the top of the hand and the wrist. Only a thin layer of leather covers the palm, which helps a player control his stick. A goalie wears two different gloves—one for catching pucks and one for blocking them. Goalies also wear heavy leg pads and a mask. They paint their masks to match their personalities and team colors.

All players wear hockey skates. The blade is curved at each end. The skate "boot" is made from metal, plastic, nylon, and either real or *synthetic* leather. Goalies wear skates that have extra protection on the toe and ankle.

Chris Kunitz wears the team's 2008–09 home uniform.

Helmet

Sweater

Gloves

Pants

Skates

We Won!

Every team that wins a Stanley Cup must overcome obstacles. The Penguins were no exception. Their first championship came at the end of a difficult 1990–91 season. Mario Lemieux had missed 21 games the year before with a sore back. When surgery failed to fix the problem, doctors told the team that he might have to sit out the entire season.

The good news was that the Penguins had plenty of talent, including veterans Paul Coffey, Bryan Trottier, Ron Francis, Joe Mullen, John Cullen, and Jiri Hrdina. They were joined by rising stars Jaromir Jagr, Kevin Stevens, and Mark Recchi. Coach Bob Johnson made his players believe they could do anything. Lemieux returned to the ice in time for the playoffs. He led the confident Penguins into the

Stanley Cup Finals against the Minnesota North Stars.

Pittsburgh won three of the first five games in the series. In Game 6, Lemieux made one of his most famous moves ever. Early in the first period, the North Stars went on the power play. Lemieux stole the puck, made three beautiful fakes that left goalie Jon Casey helpless on the ice, and then flipped the puck into the net. The Penguins roared to an 8–0 victory and brought home their first Stanley Cup.

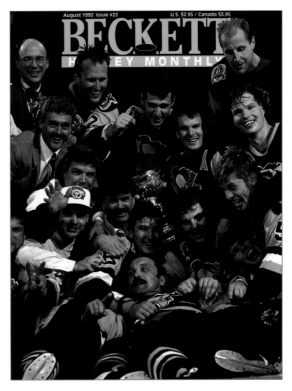

What should have been a time of celebration became a time of sorrow. Coach Johnson fell ill and died of brain cancer. Scotty Bowman, who had been working with Craig Patrick to run the club, agreed to fill in as coach for the 1991–92 season. Earlier in his career, Bowman had won four Stanley Cups in a row as coach of the Montreal Canadiens. By the 1992 **postseason**, he had the Penguins ready to defend their championship.

The Penguins met the Chicago Blackhawks in the Stanley Cup Finals. Each game in the series came down to the final moments,

LEFT: Mario Lemieux beats Jon Casey with a goal in Game 6 of the 1991 Stanley Cup Finals.   **ABOVE**: This magazine cover shows the celebration after the Penguins' 1992 Stanley Cup championship.

and each time Pittsburgh won. Other teams had captured back-to-back championships, but none could claim they had traveled the same bumpy road to get there. The Penguins had accomplished something special.

Nearly two decades passed before the Penguins returned to the Stanley Cup Finals. In the 2007–08 season, a young team led by Sidney Crosby, Evgeni Malkin, Jordan Staal, and Marc-Andre Fleury surprised many experts by reaching the championship round against the Detroit Red Wings. The Penguins lost in six games.

Pittsburgh fans still believed that the Penguins were ready to win their third Stanley Cup. But midway through the 2008–09 season, they were playing poorly. The Penguins hired Dan Bylsma to coach the team. He was young and full of energy.

The Penguins won 18 of their final 25 games and finished in second place. In the playoffs, they first defeated the Philadelphia Flyers and Washington Capitals, and then the Carolina Hurricanes in the **Eastern Conference Finals**. Each time, the Penguins won the series on the other team's home ice.

In the Stanley Cup Finals, Pittsburgh faced a rematch with Detroit. The Red Wings took the first two games at home. Game 3 was tied 2–2 in the third period. Sergei Gonchar sent a slapshot humming through a tangle of players and into the net. Pittsburgh won 4–2.

Marc-Andre Fleury stretches to make the save that sealed the 2009 Stanley Cup for the Penguins.

The Penguins had new life. They won two of the next three games to force a Game 7 showdown in Detroit. This was Fleury's chance to shine. He made save after save. Pittsburgh got its offense from Max Talbot, who scored twice in the second period.

The Penguins held a 2–1 lead as the final seconds ticked away in the third period. The Red Wings made one last attempt to tie the game. A Detroit shot hit Staal, clanked against the top of the goal, and then bounced to Nicklas Lidstrom, who was staring at a wide-open net. Fleury dove to his right and stopped Lidstrom's shot as time ran out. The Penguins were champions again!

Go-To Guys

To be a true star in the NHL, you need more than a great slapshot. You have to be a "go-to guy"—someone teammates trust to make the winning play when the seconds are ticking away in a big game. Penguins fans have had a lot to cheer about over the years, including these great stars ...

THE PIONEERS

JEAN PRONOVOST   Right Wing

• BORN: DECEMBER 18, 1945 • PLAYED FOR TEAM: 1968–69 TO 1977–78

Jean Pronovost was an excellent **all-around** player and the first Penguin to score 100 points (goals plus **assists**) in a season. In his final five years with Pittsburgh, he scored 40 or more goals four times. Whenever the team needed a big goal, Pronovost seemed to get it.

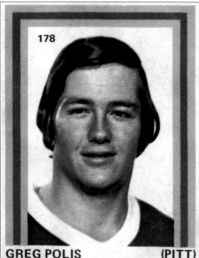

178

GREG POLIS   (PITT)

GREG POLIS   Left Wing

• BORN: AUGUST 8, 1950
• PLAYED FOR TEAM: 1970–71 TO 1973–74

The Penguins used their first pick in the 1970 draft on Greg Polis. He was a fast skater who did not mind mixing it up in the corners with bigger players. In 1973, he was named **Most Valuable Player (MVP)** of the **All-Star Game**.

ABOVE: Greg Polis   **RIGHT**: Syl Apps Jr.

SYL APPS JR.   **Center**

SYL APPS

- Born: August 1, 1947
- Played for Team: 1970–71 to 1977–78

Syl Apps Jr. was the son of a Hockey **Hall of Famer**. He made a name for himself as one of the Penguins' first stars. Apps led Pittsburgh in scoring three times.

DAVE BURROWS   **Defenseman**

- Born: January 11, 1949
- Played for Team: 1971–72 to 1977–78 & 1980–81

When Dave Burrows joined the Penguins in 1971, he found himself teamed with his childhood hero, Tim Horton. Burrows went on to become one of the best one-on-one defenders in the NHL. He could skate backward faster than many players could skate forward.

RICK KEHOE   **Right Wing**

- Born: July 15, 1951   • Played for Team: 1974–75 to 1984–85

Rick Kehoe proved you don't have to be a rough player to be a good player. He was hardly ever whistled for a penalty, yet he was always a threat to score. In 1980–81, Kehoe had 55 goals and spent only six minutes in the penalty box. He was awarded the Lady Byng Trophy for sportsmanship.

RANDY CARLYLE   **Defenseman**

- Born: April 19, 1956   • Played for Team: 1978–79 to 1983–84

The Penguins were not very good when Randy Carlyle joined them. Thanks to his strong defense and fiery leadership, they made the playoffs in each of his first four seasons with the team. In 1980–81, Carlyle won the Norris Trophy as the NHL's top defenseman.

MODERN STARS

MARIO LEMIEUX   Center

- BORN: OCTOBER 5, 1965
- PLAYED FOR TEAM: 1984–85 TO 1996–97 & 2000–01 TO 2005–06

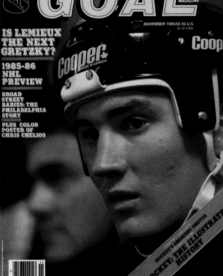

Mario Lemieux had to sit out more than 500 games due to illness and injuries. Still, he won the Hart Trophy as the NHL's best player three times and led the league in scoring six times. Lemieux finished his career with 690 goals and 1,003 assists in only 915 games.

KEVIN STEVENS   Left Wing

- BORN: APRIL 15, 1965
- PLAYED FOR TEAM: 1987–88 TO 1994–95
  & 2000–01 TO 2001–02

During Pittsburgh's championship years, Kevin Stevens was the best left wing in hockey. He topped 50 goals and 100 points two years in a row. In 1991–92, Stevens set a new record for left wings—and also for American-born players—with 123 points.

RON FRANCIS   Center

- BORN: MARCH 1, 1963   • PLAYED FOR TEAM: 1990–91 TO 1997–98

The Penguins were a good team with Mario Lemieux. They became a great team after they traded for Ron Francis. He was a brilliant passer and an unselfish player. Francis led the NHL in assists twice and became the team's leader when Lemieux was unable to play.

   ABOVE: Mario Lemieux   **RIGHT**: Sidney Crosby and Evgeni Malkin

JAROMIR JAGR — Right Wing

- BORN: FEBRUARY 15, 1972   • PLAYED FOR TEAM: 1990–91 TO 2000–01

Jaromir Jagr was sometimes overshadowed by Mario Lemieux, but teammates and opponents knew how good he was. Jagr topped 100 points four times for the Penguins and always had one of the best **plus/minus ratings** in the league. When he and Lemieux skated together, the Penguins were almost unbeatable.

SIDNEY CROSBY — Center

- BORN: AUGUST 7, 1987   • FIRST SEASON WITH TEAM: 2005–06

Sidney Crosby joined the Penguins at the age of 18 and became one of the team's leaders within a few months. As a rookie, he was the youngest player in NHL history to score 100 points. In his second year, Crosby was the youngest player ever to lead a major North American sport in scoring. That same year, Crosby won the Hart Trophy.

EVGENI MALKIN — Center

- BORN: JULY 31, 1986
- FIRST SEASON WITH TEAM: 2006–07

Evgeni Malkin played in his home country of Russia for three seasons before coming to Pittsburgh. The young star known as "Geno" was worth the wait. In 2006–07, the tall, graceful center beat out teammate Jordan Staal for the Calder Trophy as the NHL's best rookie. In 2008–09, Malkin won the Art Ross Trophy as the league's top scorer and the Conn Smythe Trophy as the best player in the playoffs.

THE GENESIS FUND

Behind the Bench

In 2009, the Penguins hired their 20th coach, Dan Bylsma. A few months later, he led Pittsburgh to the Stanley Cup. Like many of the team's coaches, Bylsma had once been an NHL player. Other former players who led the Penguins include **All-Stars** Ken Schinkel, Red Kelly, and Eddie Johnston.

The Penguins' three best coaches were Scotty Bowman, Herb Brooks, and Bob Johnson. Bowman was an NHL legend who retired with nine Stanley Cup championships. One of those came in 1992, when he led the Penguins to the top of the NHL. Brooks was just as famous. He led Team USA to a gold medal in the 1980 **Winter Olympics**—and in the famous "Miracle on Ice" victory over the Soviet Union.

Pittsburgh's most beloved coach was Johnson. He was also an Olympic legend—he coached the 1976 U.S. team and won three college championships. The Penguins hired Johnson to bring **enthusiasm** to the club in 1990–91. He always made the Penguins smile when he shouted, "It's a great day for hockey!" Johnson led Pittsburgh to its first Stanley Cup that year. Tragically, he died of cancer several months later.

Coach Bob Johnson stands tall behind the Pittsburgh bench. He was a huge favorite with the Penguins and their fans.

One Great Day

Everyone celebrates New Year's Eve differently. In 1988, Mario Lemieux celebrated in a way unmatched by anyone before or since. The Penguins were playing the New Jersey Devils in Pittsburgh. New Jersey was leading 1–0 with the teams at **even strength**. Lemieux swooped down the right side. He fired the puck against the skate of a Devils defender. The shot went past goalie Bob Sauve and into the net.

Later in the first period, New Jersey had a power play. Lemieux got the puck just as the Devils were trying to get fresh players on the ice. He tried a backhand shot that wiggled its way into the net for a short-handed goal. Later in the period, with the Penguins on the power play, Lemieux rocketed a slapshot inside the left goalpost for his third goal of the game.

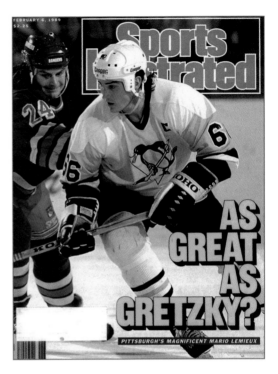

LEFT: Mario Lemieux warms up before a game.   RIGHT: After Lemieux's great game against the New Jersey Devils, national magazines wondered if he was hockey's best player ever.

The Devils replaced the shell-shocked Sauve with Chris Terreri. Moments later, Lemieux was about to skate free for a breakaway when he was pulled to the ice. The referees called for a penalty shot. Lemieux scooped up the puck at center ice and glided toward the New Jersey goal. When he saw Terreri open his leg pads, he fired the puck in between them for an easy goal.

The Devils did not give up. They made the score 7–6. As time was running out, Terreri skated to the bench to give New Jersey an extra skater. This left the goal wide open. With a few seconds left, the Penguins stole the puck and passed it to Lemieux. He flicked it into the empty net just before the final buzzer sounded.

There are five ways to score a goal in the NHL, and "Super Mario" had pulled off every one—in the same game! Lemieux scored a goal at even strength, short-handed, on the power play, on a penalty shot, and into an open net.

Legend Has It

Which NHL mascot played a movie bad guy?

LEGEND HAS IT that Iceburgh did. The Penguins' *mascot* appeared in the Jean-Claude Van Damme film *Sudden Death*. The man inside the costume was one of the movie's villains. *Sudden Death* was written by Karen Baldwin, the wife of team owner Howard Baldwin. The movie made $64 million in 1995—more than the Penguins did that year!

ABOVE: Iceburgh gets the crowd pumped up during a Penguins game.
RIGHT: An illustrated booklet about Greg Polis.

Which Penguin learned to play hockey with his dog?

THE GREG POLIS STORY

BOOKLET NO. 9

LEGEND HAS IT that Greg Polis did. Polis grew up in a **remote** prairie town in Alberta, Canada. Only 75 people lived there. In fact, there were not enough kids his age to ever get a hockey game going, so Polis would play keep-away with his Labrador retriever. Polis got so good that he soon drew the attention of **scouts** and eventually made it to the NHL.

Which Pittsburgh announcer invented his own language?

LEGEND HAS IT that Mike Lange did. In today's NHL locker rooms, you can hear English, French, Czech, Swedish, Finnish, Russian, and a few other languages. Penguins fans often get an altogether different "Lange-uage" when they tune into games. Lange is one of the most colorful announcers in hockey history. He likes to celebrate Pittsburgh goals with sayings such as "Scratch my back with a hacksaw!" and "Get that dog off my lawnmower!" and "Get in the fast lane, Grandma, the bingo game is ready to roll!" Fans love Lange, but some still have no idea what he is talking about.

It Really Happened

During his long career with the Penguins, Mario Lemieux proved again and again that he could do anything he set his mind to. He shattered one scoring record after another. He returned from diseases and injuries that would have ended almost any other player's career. After Lemieux retired and was inducted into the Hall of Fame, he came back again as Pittsburgh's owner and star player—and saved the Penguins from ***bankruptcy***.

Two days before Christmas in 2002, Pittsburgh's popular radio host Mark Madden told his listeners that he had discovered something Super Mario had never done. Although he had tried many times, Lemieux had never scored a goal from a faceoff. "I've finally found something where the greatest player in hockey looks dumb," Madden joked.

Madden also said that he would donate $6,600—Lemieux's number was 66—to the Mario Lemieux Foundation if he ever did it.

That night, Lemieux took the ice against the Buffalo Sabres. In the third period, with the score tied 2–2 and the puck in Buffalo's end, Lemieux skated into the circle to take a faceoff against Chris Gratton. The referee dropped the puck, Lemieux pulled it toward him and in

Mario Lemieux makes a pass against the Buffalo Sabres
on December 23rd, 2002.

one lightning-fast motion fired a shot at the Sabres' rookie goalie, Mika
Noronen. The puck grazed the skate of defenseman Alexei Zhitnik and
slipped between Noronen's pads. Lemieux looked up at the press box—
where he knew Madden was sitting—and smiled.

"I'm going to probably have to have a fundraiser," Madden said.
"But considering my position, I think the fans will readily contribute."

"It was a bit of Mario magic!" Buffalo coach Lindy Ruff said.

Team Spirit

The Penguins and their fans have become very close over time. The team reaches out to the people of Western Pennsylvania with many different programs. Sidney Crosby supports the Little Penguins "Learn to Play Hockey" program. He teaches kids how to skate and shoot. The team also picks fans between the ages of 7 and 12 to be Junior Reporters. They talk to players before games, and then the interviews are shown on the Jumbotron scoreboard at the Igloo.

The team's most amazing charity work happens through the Mario Lemieux Foundation. Lemieux started the organization after surviving a type of cancer called Hodgkin's Disease. Today, it raises millions of dollars for cancer research. In 2005, Lemieux presented a $2 million check to Children's Home of Pittsburgh. The team also gives out an annual $5,000 college scholarship named after Bob Johnson, the coach who led the Penguins to their first Stanley Cup.

During games, the Pittsburgh fans have fun with Iceburgh, a huge skating penguin who wears uniform number 00. He has been entertaining crowds at the Igloo since 1993. For the playoffs, fans show their team spirit by dressing in white. The view from the ice gives the players tremendous confidence and energy.

Pittsburgh's arena is a sea of white during the 2008 Stanley Cup Finals.

Timeline

The hockey season is played from October through June. That means each season takes place at the end of one year and the beginning of the next. In this timeline, the accomplishments of the Penguins are shown by season.

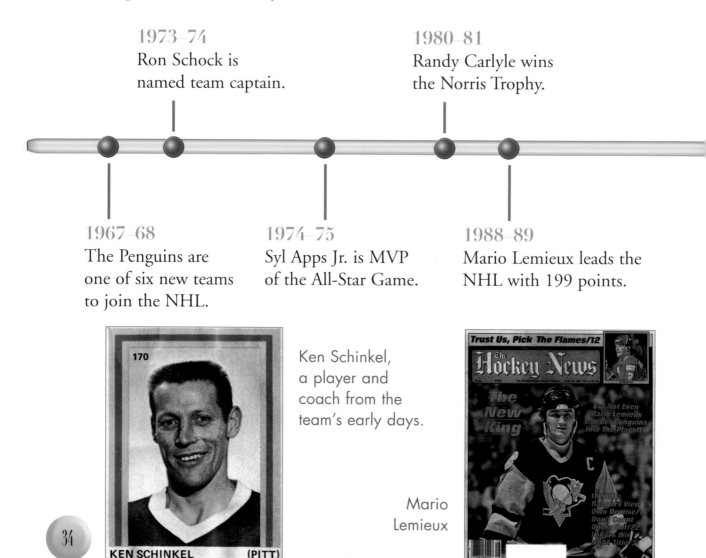

1973–74
Ron Schock is named team captain.

1980–81
Randy Carlyle wins the Norris Trophy.

1967–68
The Penguins are one of six new teams to join the NHL.

1974–75
Syl Apps Jr. is MVP of the All-Star Game.

1988–89
Mario Lemieux leads the NHL with 199 points.

170

KEN SCHINKEL   (PITT)

Ken Schinkel, a player and coach from the team's early days.

Trust Us, Pick The Flames/12

The Hockey News

The New King

But Not Even Mario Lemieux Can Get Penguins Into The Playoffs

Mario Lemieux

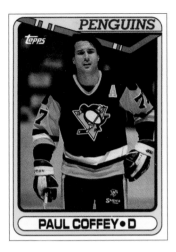

Paul Coffey, a leader for the 1991 champs.

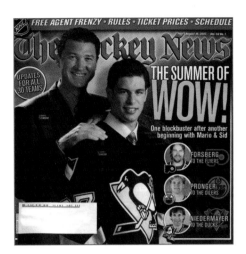

Mario Lemieux and Sidney Crosby

1991–92
The Penguins win their second Stanley Cup.

2005–06
Sidney Crosby becomes the youngest player to score 100 points.

1990–91
The Penguins win their first Stanley Cup.

2007–08
Pittsburgh reaches the Stanley Cup Finals for the third time.

2008–09
The Penguins win their third Stanley Cup.

Max Talbot celebrates with Ruslan Fedotenko after his goal that won Game 7 of the 2009 Stanley Cup Finals.

Fun Facts

HATS OFF

Jordan Staal scored his first NHL **hat trick** at the age of 18 years and 153 days. That made him the youngest player in NHL history with three goals in a game. The previous record had stood since 1943.

COLOR CODE

The Penguins switched to black-and-gold uniforms in 1980. The Boston Bruins already wore those colors and complained to the league. The Penguins pointed out that history was on their side. The Pittsburgh Pirates hockey club used black and gold during its time in the NHL in the 1920s.

WHAT A SCHOCK!

While playing for the St. Louis Blues, Ron Schock was asked at a hockey dinner which teams he would least like to play for. One of them, he said, was the Penguins. Two days later, he was traded to Pittsburgh. He played eight years for the Penguins and became one of the team's most popular players!

SIBLING RIVALS

Jean Pronovost was very good at elbowing his way out of trouble in the corners. Maybe that was because he was the 11th of 12 kids in his family. As a boy, he had to battle for almost everything he wanted. His older brother, Marcel, was an All-Star defenseman for the Detroit Red Wings and Toronto Maple Leafs.

PENGUINS

JEAN PRONOVOST   right wing

GOOD LUCK PUCK

On October 19th, 2008, Evgeni Malkin scored his 200th point and Sidney Crosby scored his 100th goal on the same play. After the game, the Penguins' trainer sawed the puck in two and gave a half to each player.

BLACKHAWKS DOWN

On October 21st, 1967, the Penguins became the first **expansion team** to beat one of the NHL's "Original Six" teams. They defeated the Chicago Blackhawks, 4–2.

LEFT: Jordan Staal   **ABOVE**: Jean Pronovost

Talking Hockey

"Obviously, you love to score goals. You love to make assists and do things like that. But at the same time, at the end of the day, you want to win."

— *Sidney Crosby, on doing the little things that make a team better*

"All that matters is that you find a way to put the puck in the net. It doesn't matter how. I learned that from Mario."

— *Jaromir Jagr, on the most important lesson that Mario Lemieux taught him*

"It was such a great feeling to hold the Cup over your head out on the ice!"

— *Mark Recchi, on winning the 1991 Stanley Cup Finals*

"All I can say to the young players is enjoy every moment of it. Just enjoy every moment of it. Your career goes by very quickly."

— *Mario Lemieux, on the special thrill of playing in the NHL*

ABOVE: Jaromir Jagr and Mario Lemieux
RIGHT: Ron Francis

"Bob Johnson was like a father to us, but we made the adjustment to Scotty Bowman."
—*Ron Francis, on winning the Stanley Cup under two very different coaches*

"We're looking at one of the best players in the world. They put him in the category of Bobby Orr. There's not too many guys like that who come around."
—*Eddie Johnston, on defenseman Paul Coffey*

"You've got to keep at it, keep on the game plan, keep wearing your opponent down."
—*Dan Bylsma, on what it takes to win the Stanley Cup*

"You win as a team, you lose as a team. I just try to do my job."
—*Marc-Andre Fleury, on the value of being a team player*

"When everybody compares me to Mario Lemieux, it's an honor."
—*Evgeni Malkin, on being compared to the greatest player in team history*

For the Record

The great Penguins teams and players have left their marks on the record books. These are the "best of the best" ...

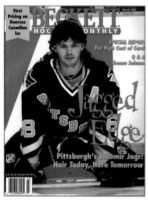

Jaromir Jagr

Sidney Crosby

PENGUINS AWARD WINNERS

HART MEMORIAL TROPHY
MOST VALUABLE PLAYER (MVP)

Mario Lemieux	1987–88
Mario Lemieux	1992–93
Mario Lemieux	1995–96
Jaromir Jagr	1998–99
Sidney Crosby	2006–07

ALL-STAR GAME MVP

Greg Polis	1972–73
Syl Apps Jr.	1974–75
Mario Lemieux	1984–85
Mario Lemieux	1987–88
Mario Lemieux	1989–90

JAMES NORRIS MEMORIAL TROPHY
TOP DEFENSIVE PLAYER

Randy Carlyle	1980–81

CALDER TROPHY
TOP ROOKIE PLAYER

Mario Lemieux	1984–85
Evgeni Malkin	2006–07

ART ROSS TROPHY
TOP SCORER

Mario Lemieux	1987–88
Mario Lemieux	1988–89
Mario Lemieux	1991–92
Mario Lemieux	1992–93
Jaromir Jagr	1994–95
Mario Lemieux	1995–96
Mario Lemieux	1996–97
Jaromir Jagr	1997–98
Jaromir Jagr	1998–99
Jaromir Jagr	1999–00
Jaromir Jagr	2000–01
Sidney Crosby	2006–07
Evgeni Malkin	2008–09

CONN SMYTHE TROPHY
MVP DURING PLAYOFFS

Mario Lemieux	1990–91
Mario Lemieux	1991–92
Evgeni Malkin	2008–09

A pennant celebrating the team's 2008 conference championship.

PENGUINS ACHIEVEMENTS

ACHIEVEMENT	SEASON
Stanley Cup Champions	1990–91
Stanley Cup Champions	1991–92
Stanley Cup Finalists	2007–08
Stanley Cup Champions	2008–09

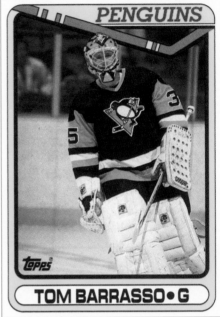

PENGUINS

Topps

TOM BARRASSO • G

ABOVE: Tom Barrasso, the goalie for the Penguins during their runs to the Stanley Cup in 1991 and 1992.

LEFT: Mario Lemieux takes a faceoff. He has won more awards than any other Penguin.

Pinpoints

T he history of a hockey team is made up of many smaller stories. These stories take place all over the map—not just in the city a team calls "home." Match the pushpins on these maps to the Team Facts and you will begin to see the story of the Penguins unfold!

TEAM FACTS

1 Pittsburgh, Pennsylvania—*The Penguins have played here since 1967–68.*

2 Brockton, Massachusetts—*Kevin Stevens was born here.*

3 Grand Haven, Michigan—*Dan Bylsma was born here.*

4 Minneapolis, Minnesota—*Bob Johnson was born here.*

5 Sacramento, California—*Mike Lange was born here.*

6 Cole Harbour, Nova Scotia, Canada—*Sidney Crosby was born here.*

7 Taschereau, Quebec, Canada—*Pierre Larouche was born here.*

8 Sorel-Tracy, Quebec, Canada—*Marc-Andre Fleury was born here.*

9 Jansen, Saskatchewan, Canada—*Ken Schinkel was born here.*

10 Westlock, Alberta, Canada—*Greg Polis was born here.*

11 Kladno, Czech Republic*—*Jaromir Jagr was born here.*

12 Magnitogorsk, Russia—*Evgeni Malkin was born here.*

The Czech Republic was formerly Czechoslovakia.

Pierre
Larouche

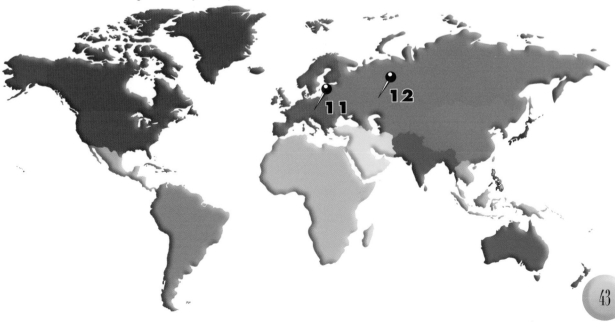

43

Faceoff

Hockey is played between two teams of five skaters and a goalie. Each team has two defensemen and a forward line that includes a left wing, right wing, and center. The goalie's job is to stop the puck from crossing the red goal line. A hockey goal is 6 feet (1.8 meters) wide and 4 feet (1.2 meters) high. The hockey puck is a round disk made of hard rubber. It weighs approximately 6 ounces.

During a game, players work hard for a full "shift." When they get tired, they take a seat on the bench, and a new group jumps off the bench and over the boards to take their place (except for the goalie). Forwards play together in set groups, or "lines," and defensemen do, too.

There are rules that prevent players from injuring or interfering with opponents. However, players are allowed to bump, or "check," each other when they battle for the puck. Because hockey is a fast game played by strong athletes, sometimes checks can be rough!

If a player breaks a rule, a penalty is called by one of two referees. For most penalties, the player must sit in the penalty box for two minutes. This gives the other team a one-skater advantage, or "power play." The team down a skater is said to be "short-handed."

NHL games have three 20-minute periods—60 minutes in all—and the team that scores the most goals is the winner. If the score is tied, the teams play an overtime period. The first team to score during overtime wins. If the game is still tied, it is decided by a shootout—a one-on-one

contest between the goalies and the best shooters from the other team. During the Stanley Cup playoffs, no shootouts are held. The teams play until the tie is broken.

Things happen so quickly in hockey that it is easy to overlook set plays. The next time you watch a game, see if you can spot these plays:

PLAY LIST

DEFLECTION—Sometimes a shooter does not try to score a goal. Instead, he aims his shot so that a teammate can touch the puck with his stick and suddenly change its direction. If the goalie is moving to stop the first shot, he may be unable to adjust to the "deflection."

GIVE-AND-GO—When a skater is closely guarded and cannot get an open shot, he sometimes passes to a teammate with the idea of getting a return pass in better position to shoot. The "give-and-go" works when the defender turns to follow the pass and loses track of his man. By the time he recovers, it is too late.

ONE-TIMER—When a player receives a pass, he often has to control the puck and position himself for a shot. This gives the defense a chance to react. Some players are skilled enough to shoot the instant a pass arrives for a "one-timer." A well-aimed one-timer is almost impossible to stop.

PULLING THE GOALIE—Sometimes in the final moments of a game, the team that is behind will try a risky play. To gain an extra skater, the team will pull the goalie out of the game and replace him with a center, wing, or defenseman. This gives the team a better chance to score. It also leaves the goal unprotected and allows the opponent a chance to score an "empty-net goal."

Glossary

HOCKEY WORDS TO KNOW

ALL-AROUND—Good at all parts of the game.

ALL-STAR GAME—The annual game featuring the NHL's best players. Prior to 1967, the game was played at the beginning of the season between the league champion and an All-Star squad. Today it is played during the season. The game doesn't count in the standings.

ALL-STARS—Players recognized as the league's best at the end of each season.

ASSISTS—Passes that lead to a goal.

DRAFT CHOICES—Selections in the NHL draft each summer.

EASTERN CONFERENCE FINALS—The series that determines which team from the East will face the best team from the West in the Stanley Cup Finals.

EVEN STRENGTH—When both teams have five skaters and a goalie on the ice.

EXPANSION TEAM—A new team added to a league.

HALL OF FAMER—A player who has been honored as being among the greatest ever and is enshrined in the Hockey Hall of Fame.

HAT TRICK—Three goals in one game.

MINOR-LEAGUE—A level of play below the NHL.

MOST VALUABLE PLAYER (MVP)—The award given to the best player in the All-Star Game.

NATIONAL HOCKEY LEAGUE (NHL)—The league that began play in 1917–18 and is still in existence today.

PLAYMAKER—A player who creates scoring opportunities.

PLAYOFFS—The games played after the season to determine the league champion.

PLUS/MINUS RATINGS—A statistic that measures a player's effectiveness by comparing the goals scored for and against his team when he's on the ice.

POSTSEASON—Another term for playoffs.

ROLE PLAYERS—Players who have a specific job when they are on the ice.

ROOKIES—Players in their first season.

SCOUTS—People who watch young players and decide if they are good enough to play professionally.

SHUTOUTS—Games in which a team is prevented from scoring.

STANLEY CUP—The championship trophy of North American hockey since 1893, and of the NHL since 1927.

STANLEY CUP FINALS—The series that determines the NHL champion each season. It has been a best-of-seven series since 1939.

VETERANS—Players with great experience.

OTHER WORDS TO KNOW

BANKRUPTCY—A situation where a business does not have the money to pay its bills.

CLASSIC—Popular for a long time.

DECADES—Periods of 10 years; also specific periods, such as the 1950s.

EMERGING—Quickly improving.

ENTHUSIASM—Strong excitement.

ERA—A period of time in history.

EXPERIENCED—Having knowledge and skill in a job.

GENERATION—A group of people born during the same period of history.

LOGO—A symbol or design that represents a company or team.

MASCOT—An animal or person believed to bring a group good luck.

REMARKABLE—Unusual or exceptional.

REMOTE—Far removed from anything else.

RETRACTABLE—Able to pull back.

STRATEGY—A plan or method for succeeding.

SYNTHETIC—Made in a laboratory, not in nature.

WINTER OLYMPICS—An international sports competition held every four years.

Places to Go

ON THE ROAD

PITTSBURGH PENGUINS
66 Mario Lemieux Place
Pittsburgh, Pennsylvania 15219
(412) 642-1300

THE HOCKEY HALL OF FAME
Brookfield Place
30 Yonge Street
Toronto, Ontario, Canada   M5E 1X8
(416) 360-7765

ON THE WEB

THE NATIONAL HOCKEY LEAGUE   www.nhl.com
  • *Learn more about the National Hockey League*

THE PITTSBURGH PENGUINS   penguins.nhl.com
  • *Learn more about the Penguins*

THE HOCKEY HALL OF FAME   www.hhof.com
  • *Learn more about hockey's greatest players*

ON THE BOOKSHELF

To learn more about the sport of hockey, look for these books at your library or bookstore:

  • MacDonald, James. *Hockey Skills: How to Play Like a Pro*. Berkeley Heights, New Jersey: Enslow Elementary, 2009.

  • Keltie, Thomas. *Inside Hockey! The legends, facts, and feats that made the game*. Toronto, Ontario, Canada: Maple Tree Press, 2008.

  • Romanuk, Paul. *Scholastic Canada Book of Hockey Lists*. Markham, Ontario, Canada: Scholastic Canada, 2007.

Index

PAGE NUMBERS IN **BOLD** REFER TO ILLUSTRATIONS.

The Team

MARK STEWART has written over 200 books for kids—and more than a dozen books on hockey, including a history of the Stanley Cup and an authorized biography of goalie Martin Brodeur. He grew up in New York City during the 1960s rooting for the Rangers and now lives in New Jersey, where he attends Devils games at the new Prudential Center. He especially likes the special all-you-can-eat seating section. Mark comes from a family of writers. His grandfather was Sunday Editor of *The New York Times* and his mother was Articles Editor of *The Ladies' Home Journal* and *McCall's*. Mark has profiled hundreds of athletes over the last 20 years. He has also written several books about New York and New Jersey. Mark is a graduate of Duke University, with a degree in History. He lives with his daughters and wife Sarah overlooking Sandy Hook, New Jersey.

DENIS GIBBONS is a writer and editor with *The Hockey News* and a former newsletter editor of the Toronto-based Society for International Hockey Research (SIHR). He was a contributing writer to the publication *Kings of the Ice: A History of World Hockey* and has worked as chief hockey researcher at five Winter Olympics for the ABC, CBS, and NBC television networks. Denis also has worked as a researcher for the FOX Sports Network during the Stanley Cup playoffs. He resides in Burlington, Ontario, Canada with his wife Chris.

WITHDRAWN